Fly High!

THE STORY OF BESSIE COLEMAN

by LOUISE BORDEN *and* MARY KAY KROEGER

illustrated by TERESA FLAVIN

MARGARET K. MCELDERRY BOOKS
NEW YORK • LONDON • TORONTO • SYDNEY • SINGAPORE

ALSO BY LOUISE BORDEN

THE LITTLE SHIPS
THE HEROIC RESCUE AT DUNKIRK IN WORLD WAR II
illustrated by Michael Foreman

GOOD-BYE, CHARLES LINDBERGH
illustrated by Thomas B. Allen

GOOD LUCK, MRS. K.!
illustrated by Adam Gustavson

THE SLEDS ON BOSTON COMMON
A STORY FROM THE AMERICAN REVOLUTION
illustrated by Robert Andrew Parker

The authors would like to thank Marion Coleman for sharing with us personal recollections of her Aunt Bessie, and Doris L. Rich, author of *Queen Bess, Daredevil Aviator,* Smithsonian Institute Press, 1993, for her generous help and counsel regarding the biographical and historical accuracy of our text. Warm thanks also are due to Catie Borden, the Chicago Historical Society, the Chicago Public Library, and to Donna Marsh, whose encouragement started us on our research road back in 1993.

Margaret K. McElderry Books
An imprint of Simon & Schuster Children's Publishing Division
1230 Avenue of the Americas
New York, New York 10020
Text copyright © 2001 by Louise Borden and Mary Kay Kroeger
Illustrations copyright © 2001 by Teresa Flavin
All rights reserved, including the right of reproduction in whole or in part in any form.
Book design by Angela Carlino
The text of this book was set in LinoLetter Medium.
The illustrations were rendered in gouache on colored paper.
Printed in Hong Kong
1 2 3 4 5 6 7 8 9 10

Library of Congress Cataloging-in-Publication Data
Borden, Louise. Fly high!: the story of Bessie Coleman / Louise Borden and Mary Kay Kroeger; illustrated by Teresa Flavin. p. cm.
Summary: Discusses the life of the determined African American woman who went all the way to France in order to earn her pilot's license in 1921.
ISBN 0-689-82457-2
1. Coleman, Bessie, 1896–1926—Juvenile literature. 2. Afro-American women air pilots—Biography—Juvenile literature. [1. Coleman, Bessie, 1896–1926. 2. Air pilots. 3. Afro-Americans—Biography. 4. Women—Biography.] I. Kroeger, Mary Kay. II. Flavin, Teresa, ill. III. Title.
TL540.C646B67   2000   629.13'092—dc21   [b]   99-17398

FIRST
EDITION

EARLY YEARS

A hundred years ago in Waxahachie, Texas,
Bessie Coleman walked four miles to her one-room schoolhouse
and four miles home.
Bessie loved numbers.
And learning numbers was worth walking those long, dusty miles
past tenant farms and cotton fields and small, shabby houses.

Bessie Coleman was a reader, too.
Twice a year,
a library wagon stopped in front of
her small home on Palmer Road.
And twice a year,
Bessie's mother, Susan Coleman, used her ironing money
to rent books for Bessie to read . . .
books about people whose skin was the color of Bessie's . . .
people like Harriet Tubman and Booker T. Washington.
They were *somebody,* all right.

Susan Coleman had been just ten years old
when the Civil War ended.
The daughter of Georgia slaves,
she couldn't read or write,
but she had a big heart
and spoke with kind words.
Susan knew how to plant seeds,
pick cotton, and teach her children to love God.

Many times at the end of those long days,
Bessie stood next to the head foreman,
checking his numbers.
She wanted to make sure that the cotton her family had picked
was weighed fair and square.
Susan Coleman had a proud smile when she saw her Bessie
write down those numbers and figure out the sums.
Someday, that girl would be *somebody*.

From the start,
Bessie Coleman had always been a walker and a counter.
Now, as she grew older, Bessie was a dreamer.
On Saturdays,
Bessie walked five miles across the streets of Waxahachie
taking clean shirts to the big houses of folks who had money.
And Bessie walked five miles home to her sisters and her mom
with another sack of laundry to wash and press.
Maybe if she saved enough ironing money,
she could get a better education . . .
beyond the skimpy eight grades in that one-room schoolhouse.
With more schooling, she could be *somebody*.
Several years later,
at the age of eighteen,
Bessie took catch-up classes at a university in Oklahoma.*
The students there in Langston had dark skin, too.
Bessie was placed in the sixth grade.
But the classes cost too much for a country girl.
After only one term,
Bessie had to come back home
to the three-room house on Palmer Road.

* This was the Colored Agricultural and Normal University.

CHICAGO YEARS

"Chicago! Head north! There are jobs for all!"
Lots of folks from the South heard those words.
Maybe Walter, an older brother,
could help Bessie find a bigger life there.
Walter was somebody.
He had moved to Chicago years before when Bessie was little.
Now Walter was a fine Pullman porter.

It was Bessie's time to try again.

She was twenty-three years old when she moved to Chicago.

The year was 1915,

a busy time for the big, big city up north.

Chicago had tall buildings

and trains

and streetcars.

The wide sidewalks were full of talk and news.

Chicago had the wind off Lake Michigan,

and deep winter snows,

and was miles away

from the dirt-floor cabin where Bessie had been born.

In Chicago, you could be *somebody*.

Now Bessie needed a job.
There were many barbershops in South Chicago.
And most of them had a manicurist.
Bessie knew she could learn how to trim and file nails.
It was a lot easier than picking cotton!
If she were fast at it, she could make good money.
And that's just what Bessie did.
First she worked in a shop on State Street,
then she moved to Duncan's Barbershop on East Thirty-sixth.
While Bessie clipped and filed nails,
she listened to Chicago baseball talk
and the deep voices and stories of men.

Big city life was new,
and it was fun.
Bessie was still a reader.
Every day she read the pages of the *Chicago Defender*,
a newspaper for *her* people published by Robert Abbott.
Robert Abbott was *somebody*, and his work was news.

Bessie wrote letters of her life in Chicago back to Texas.
Soon the rest of the Coleman family moved north, to the big,
    windy city.

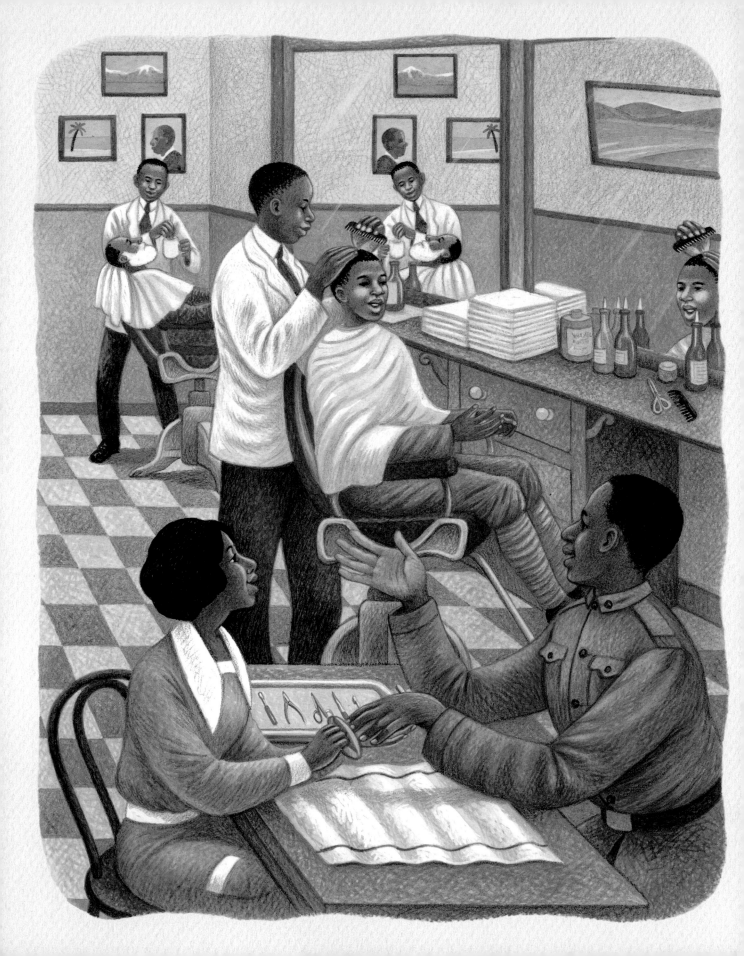

In the fall of 1919,
Duncan's was abuzz with the stories of soldiers
who had fought in the trenches of France.
Bessie's brothers Walter and John had served in that war, too.
Now they were back in Chicago,
home safe and sound
from the battles of World War I.
Bessie Coleman was a good listener.
As she filed and buffed her customers' nails
near the front window of the shop,
Bessie heard tales of French women who could fly airplanes.
John Coleman told Bessie:
"Those French lady pilots, they are *somebody*."

OFF TO FRANCE

From then on, Bessie wanted to fly.
The pilots and aviators in Abbott's *Chicago Defender*
led exciting lives.
If they could learn to fly, so could she.
All she needed was a good teacher.

But Bessie was a woman,
a woman with dark skin.
And she didn't have much money.
The only pilots in Chicago were men, white men.
Not one of them would teach her to fly a plane.
But Bessie Coleman,
who had walked four miles to school and back to learn her
    numbers,
who had walked five miles and back to earn money,
didn't give up her plan to learn how to fly.
Someday she would be a *somebody* on Chicago's South Side.
Robert Abbott would know a teacher.
Robert Abbott was the man to see.

"You can learn to fly in France," Abbott told Bessie.
"If you earn some money and learn to speak French,
then I'll help you find a flying school."

Bessie worked and saved and saved and worked.
One day she placed a toy airplane,
made by a neighborhood boy,
in the window of Duncan's Barbershop.
Bessie Coleman told herself,
"Someday *I'll* be a pilot, small step by small step."

To make better wages,
Bessie left the barbershop to work in a chili restaurant.
Now that she had more money to put in the bank,
Bessie signed up to take French classes on Michigan Avenue.
"Bonjour . . . Au revoir . . . C'est la vie . . ."
Bessie said the new French words over and over
in her kitchen as she cooked for her nieces and nephews.
She was the favorite aunt who let them
play records on her windup Victrola.
She even gave them money for movies.
Young Arthur and Marion and the other Coleman cousins
thought their Aunt Bessie was the best aunt in town.

On a November day in 1920,
Bessie boarded the S.S. *Imperator* from a New York City pier
and sailed for France.
She had her passport in her pocket
and some money from her friend Robert Abbott.
Bessie Coleman was twenty-eight years old.

In a small town near the Somme River,
two Frenchmen ran a famous flying school.
Yes, they would teach Bessie how to fly.
For seven months, in a country far from the cotton fields of Texas,
Bessie walked nine miles to the airfield,
and nine miles home to the village of Rue.
She had no friends to help her,
no family.
But she wanted to learn to fly.

And fly she did!
Just like the pilots in the news stories of the *Chicago Defender*.
Just like the pilots in the United States
who were men and who were white.
Bessie Coleman learned the same skills that they knew
with courage in her heart.
Now Bessie knew all the words—in French and in English—
for the parts of the small plane she was learning to fly:
cockpit, rudder bar, stick, and struts.
She heard the stories about other pilots
who crashed their fragile planes,
who sometimes lost their lives.
But still she kept walking those long miles to the airfield.
Nine miles to her French biplane,
whose wings were made of cloth.
And nine miles back to her room in Rue.

She would fly high, and be *somebody*.
And tell others of her race that they could do the same thing, too.

On June 15, 1921,
Bessie Coleman put an important piece of paper in her pocket—
an international license to fly.
It was the very best license to have:
With it, Bessie could fly *anywhere* in the world.
Nobody could say, "You're a Negro woman, you can't fly."
Bessie then headed to Paris
and bought a fancy leather coat.
Now she was an aviatrix,
a *très chic!* aviatrix.

Back Home in the U.S.A.

That September, Bessie Coleman sailed back to New York Harbor.
Now she was news, front-page news.
African-American newspapers all over the country
had stories about the first person of their race
to learn to fly.

Always waving,
always smiling,
Bessie Coleman was an aviatrix with spunk and style.

Eager to improve her flying skills for future air shows,
Bessie returned to Europe the next February.
For six months, she took more lessons in France, Germany, and
    Holland.
Tailspins! Banking turns! Figure eights! Looping the loop!

Then she came home to the U.S.
to perform all those daring stunts.
Her first air show was on Long Island
on September 3, 1922,
and "Brave Bess" was a hit!

Bessie drew big crowds whenever she flew.
Petite and pretty
even in a leather helmet and goggles,
Bessie wore tall, shiny boots,
and, of course,
her long coat from Paris.

In Texas, in Tennessee, in New York, in Illinois,
Bessie Coleman told her many fans:
"All of us are created equal."
If others of her race weren't allowed to buy tickets for the air shows,
then Bessie refused to fly.
Bessie Coleman was a thinker and a talker.
She visited dozens of black schools and churches in many states:
"You can be *somebody*. You can fly high, just like me."

Now Bessie wanted to help other people.
She wanted to open a flying school so that others could learn to fly.

Not everything was easy for Bessie.
Money was still a problem.
It was hard to make money flying.
And Bessie had to borrow planes to fly in.
Finally Bessie was able to buy her own plane.
Her "Jenny" was a biplane.
It wasn't new.
It was old and shabby.
But it was hers.
Then Bessie was in a terrible crash in California.
Shortly after takeoff from Santa Monica,
the Jenny's motor stalled*
and nose-dived to the ground.
Bessie was in the hospital for three long months,
and didn't fly for a year.
With the loss of her own Jenny,
Bessie again had to borrow planes for her air shows.
Most of the planes were old and not very safe.
Bessie knew that flying was a risk.
But she thought it was an important risk to take
on behalf of her race.

* In the 1920s, engine failure after takeoff was a common occurrence. The crash of
Bessie's plane was the fourth such crash in the Los Angeles area in less than a month.

A SAD ENDING

On April 29, 1926,
Bessie Coleman was in Jacksonville, Florida,
hundreds of miles away from Waxahachie,
and hundreds more away from Chicago.
She was thirty-four years old
and close to her dream of opening a flying school.
That day,
Bessie visited every African-American school in the city.
She told young people her story.
She told them: "You can do something with your life, too."
Many of Bessie's fans had tickets for her air show on May 1.
Even her friend, Robert Abbott, happened to be in town,
and when Bessie saw him in a restaurant,
she thanked her friend for giving her the chance to fly.

The day before Bessie was to fly high for the Jacksonville crowd,
she and a Texas mechanic, William Wills,
were to take a test run in the old, shabby plane that Bessie was
    to use.
That morning, Bessie knelt by her plane and said a quiet prayer.
Then she let Wills take the controls,
while she sat in the rear seat.
Bessie was a safe pilot,
but this time she didn't fasten her seat belt.
She wanted to get a better view of the land below.
Suddenly,
something was wrong!
The plane went into a tailspin.

Bessie fell from her plane, down, down, thousands of feet.
William Wills died too, after the plane crashed on the ground.
No one could believe the awful news.
Brave Bess,
who had come so many miles from the cotton fields of Texas,
would never be able to fly again,
would never be able to tell others,
"You can be *somebody,* too."

Good-bye to Brave Bess

In Jacksonville, five thousand people,
many of whom had heard Bessie's inspiring words,
came to the memorial service to say good-bye.
Then Bessie's casket went to Chicago on a train.
Up and down State Street
there were prayers and tears.
A formal funeral was held at the Pilgrim Baptist Church
in the big, big city whose streets Bessie called home.
Ten thousand people passed by her coffin to pay their respects.
They would never forget that
their Bessie Coleman had shown the world
how anyone could fly high.
Their Bessie was *somebody,* all right.

Daughter . . . aunt . . . walker . . . reader . . . dreamer . . . thinker . . .
student . . . pilot . . . speaker . . . teacher:
Bessie Coleman was all of these.
Like her mother, Susan,
Bessie knew how to plant seeds.
Her work in schools and churches
was as important as her daring spins and loops in the sky.
Across the U.S.,
some of Bessie's young fans grew up to be pilots.
Many others would remember her courage,
her smile, and her words:
"You can do something, too.
Keep trying! Fly high!"

Authors' Note:

Bessie Coleman was born in a one-room cabin in Atlanta, Texas, on January 26, 1892. Soon the Coleman family moved to Waxahachie, Texas, where Bessie lived her childhood years. The tenth of thirteen Coleman children, Bessie became the first African-American to earn a pilot's license. This license was issued by the prestigious Fédération Aéronautique Internationale.

Bessie Coleman is buried in Lincoln Cemetery in Chicago. Every spring, Bessie's achievements are honored when pilots fly high above her grave and drop wreaths from the sky. A busy street near Chicago's O'Hare Airport and a Chicago public library now bear her name.

On April 27, 1995, a commemorative stamp was issued by the United States Postal Service in honor of Bessie Coleman. This national distinction is a deserved tribute to a woman who proved that grand dreams can become a glorious reality.

"I FOUND A BRAND-NEW WORLD IN THE WRITTEN WORD."

—BESSIE COLEMAN